INVESTING IN YOUR VALUES

How to Align Your Money
with Your Beliefs and Build
a Better Future

Frank E. James

CONTENT

INTRODUCTION

For many individuals, investing in the stock market may be a frightening job, but it can also be a powerful weapon for bringing about positive change in the world. By investing in firms that share your beliefs and avoiding those that don't, you can make a real impact in the world while simultaneously earning a profit.

This book will walk you through the process of investing in your values, giving you practical advice and techniques for building a portfolio that represents your beliefs and promotes a more sustainable and ethical future.

CHAPTER ONE

Understanding Your Values

Many people nowadays want to invest their money in ways that reflect their particular views. Whether it's supporting sustainable and environmentally friendly practices, promoting social justice, or avoiding corporations that engage in unethical behavior, investing in your values may be a powerful way to promote good change in the world while simultaneously reaching your financial objectives.

In this chapter, we will look at why investing in your values is essential, how to determine your fundamental values and the significance of values in investment decision-making.

Why It's Crucial to Invest in Your Values

Putting money into your ideals is crucial for many reasons. It enables you to first and foremost support businesses that share your ideals and values while avoiding those that don't.

Allocating money to companies that are dedicated to sustainable and ethical practices, can aid in fostering positive change in the world.

Second, investing in your values may assist you in achieving both your financial and personal objectives. You might feel more connected to your assets and be more likely to hold them for the long run if you invest in businesses that share your beliefs. Investing in businesses that are well-positioned for long-term growth, can also help you get higher financial returns.

Last but not least, investing in your values might help you lead a more meaningful and rewarding life. It may feel tremendously satisfying and exciting to invest in businesses that share your ideals since you will feel as though you are changing the world for the better.

Understanding Your Core Values

A crucial first step in investing in your values is figuring out what they are. Your core values are the underlying precepts and ideas that direct your conduct and choices. These represent your top priorities and the areas where you won't make concessions.

Your basic values can be determined in a variety of ways. Consideration of the experiences and circumstances in your life that have had the most significance and influence is one approach to start. Consider the instances in your life when you were the happiest and most content, and attempt to pinpoint the guiding principles that were present at those times.

Thinking about the things you are most passionate about will help you determine your basic values. What topics and causes are most important to you? What ideals are required to build the sort of world that you wish to live in?

Next, consider the traits that people possess that you find most admirable to determine your fundamental values. How can you apply the principles you observe in the individuals you respect and admire to your own life?

The Values-Based Approach to Investment Decision-Making

While making financial selections, it's crucial to keep your basic principles in mind once you've defined them. Choosing which businesses to invest in and which to avoid might be influenced by your ideals.

Using environmental, social, and governance (ESG) criteria to assess possible investments is one method to include your values in investment decision-making.

The environmental, social, and governance policies of a corporation may be evaluated using ESG criteria, which are a set of non-financial considerations.

You may find businesses that share your values and avoid those that don't by utilizing ESG criteria. For instance, you may decide to invest in businesses that support social justice, have sound environmental regulations, and use ethical business methods.

Investing in organizations that are actively addressing the issues that are important to you is another approach to incorporating your values into the decision-making process. If you are concerned about climate change, for instance, you can decide to invest in businesses that are advancing renewable energy sources or attempting to lessen their carbon impact.

It's critical to take into account the possible risks and benefits of your investment choices in addition to using ESG standards and selecting businesses that share your values. By evaluating the financial and other

CHAPTER TWO

Creating a Values-Based Portfolio

Investing in businesses that share your beliefs may be a potent approach to advance both your financial and social objectives. This chapter will cover methods for finding businesses that share your beliefs, assessing the environmental, social, and governance (ESG) aspects of possible investments, and creating a diverse portfolio that represents your values.

How to Find Businesses that Share Your Values

It might be difficult to identify businesses that share your beliefs, but several ways can assist you in finding the ideal assets for your portfolio.

Researching businesses that are innovators in the fields you care about could be a good place to start. For instance, if you have a significant interest in environmentally friendly energy sources, you may look into businesses that are creating cutting-edge renewable energy technology or that have strict environmental regulations.

Searching for businesses that are making an effort to solve the issues that are important to you is another tactic. For instance, if you are enthusiastic about social justice, you may search for businesses that value inclusion and diversity or that are tackling economic inequality.

Also, you may utilize screening tools to find businesses that share your beliefs. Screening methods can assist you in excluding businesses that follow ideals that conflict with your own, such as those who manufacture cigarette goods or use unethical labor practices.

Assessing Prospective Investments' Environmental, Social, and Governance (ESG) Aspects

It's crucial to assess the ESG elements of those businesses after you've found possible investments that reflect your beliefs.

ESG factors are a group of non-financial variables that may be used to evaluate a company's governance processes, as well as its environmental and social effects. Typical ESG variables include:

1. Environmental impact: This covers elements like the carbon footprint, water use, and waste management techniques of a corporation.

2. Social impact: This encompasses aspects like how an organization treats its employees, community involvement, and client pleasure.

3. The company's board structure, CEO salary, and shareholder rights are some examples of governance methods.

You may find businesses that are compatible with your beliefs and well-suited for long-term success by evaluating these variables.

Developing a Diverse Portfolio that Reflects Your Values

It's time to create a diverse portfolio that matches your beliefs once you've selected the businesses that share your values and assessed their ESG performance.

For risk management and long-term investing performance, diversification is a crucial technique. A diverse portfolio should have holdings in a range of industries, geographies, and asset classes, as well as a combination of stocks, bonds, and other forms of assets.

It's crucial to weigh the risks and rewards of each investment when creating a values-based portfolio and to make sure that it is well-diversified. Your ideas and your financial objectives might need to be traded off in certain ways, but if you design your portfolio carefully and strategically, you can achieve both.

A potent strategy to accomplish your financial objectives and make a difference in the world is to invest in businesses that share your beliefs. You can make a difference in the world and succeed as an investor over the long term by finding businesses that support your beliefs, analyzing their ESG aspects, and constructing a diverse portfolio that represents your ideals.

CHAPTER THREE

Getting Around Impact Investing's Complexities

In addition to generating financial rewards, impact investing seeks to have a beneficial social or environmental impact. Impact investing has the potential to be an effective instrument for bringing about positive change in the world, but it can also be difficult and complex.

We will examine how impact investing differs from standard investing in this chapter, as well as the difficulties associated with evaluating impact and methods for locating potential impact investment possibilities.

The Distinction Between Impact Investment and Conventional Investing

The purpose of the investment is the main distinction between impact investing and standard investing. Impact investments aim to provide beneficial social or environmental results in addition to financial returns, whereas traditional investments only aim to produce financial returns for investors.

Investments in social enterprises, neighborhood improvement initiatives, and environmentally friendly businesses are just a few examples of the many diverse ways impact investments may be made. Impact investors may aim to accomplish a variety of goals, like lowering poverty, expanding access to healthcare, or fostering environmental sustainability.

It can be difficult to negotiate the complexity of this form of investment, even while impact investing has the potential to be a potent weapon for bringing about great change in the world.

The Difficulties in Assessing Effect

Measuring a project's social or environmental impact is one of the main issues faced by impact investors. Impact investments need a distinct set of measures to be measured to compare to traditional investments, which can be assessed using financial indicators like return on investment and earnings per share.

Since it frequently involves a long-term perspective and a thorough grasp of the social and environmental challenges being addressed, measuring the effect can be difficult. Moreover, the effect may be indirect or diffuse and may not necessarily lend itself to a precise quantitative assessment, making it challenging to quantify.

Notwithstanding these obstacles, quantifying the effect is essential for determining whether impact investments were successful and for ensuring that the consequences of investments are favorable for both investors and society at large.

Finding Opportunities for Impact Investing

Finding chances for impact investments can be difficult, but several ways can assist investors in finding the best possibilities for their portfolio.

Working with impact investment funds or organizations that are experts in finding and assessing impact investments is one tactic. These groups can give investors access to a variety of impact investments and assist in assessing the social and environmental effects of such investments.

Finding employment in fields that connect with your beliefs and experience is another tactic. If you have a strong interest in sustainable agriculture, for instance, you may search for impact investments in this industry.

Ultimately, before making a choice, it's critical to assess the financial and social rewards of impact investment. While an investment's social or environmental effect is vital, it is equally necessary to make sure that the investment is financially sound and can provide investors with a return.

Together with financial gains, impact investment has the potential to be a potent instrument for achieving favorable social or environmental results. Impact investment, however, necessitates a distinct set of measurements to assess its impact and can be difficult and complex. You can navigate the complexities of impact investing and accomplish both your financial and social goals by working with impact investment funds or organizations, identifying opportunities in fields that align with your values and expertise, and evaluating the financial and social returns of impact investment.

CHAPTER FOUR

Getting Over Common Obstacles

Impact investing may be a potent tool for integrating your financial objectives with your moral and ethical principles. While looking for impact investments, investors may encounter several frequent difficulties. In this chapter, we will look at how to cope with contradictory values, how to combine financial goals with social and environmental aims, and how to avoid engaging in unethical marketing practices like greenwashing.

Putting social and environmental goals and financial goals in balance

Finding a balance between financial aims and social and environmental objectives is one of the main problems of impact investing. Impact investments may not necessarily be the most financially rewarding investments, but they may still have significant social and environmental effects.

Approaching impact investment from a long-term view is crucial to overcoming this difficulty. Impact investments might not yield large financial returns right once, but they might be more reliable and sustainable in the long run.

In addition, it's crucial to consider both the financial and societal benefits of an investment. It's important to take into account an investment's social and environmental effects in addition to its financial rewards when analyzing it.

How to Handle Conflicting Values

Dealing with opposing values is another difficulty in impact investment. For instance, a potential investor could be drawn to a business that prioritizes environmental sustainability but also has a track record of violating labor laws.

It's critical to establish a defined set of principles and standards for assessing possible investments to overcome this difficulty. You may more quickly find investments that support your principles and steer clear of those that do not by being clear about your values and criteria.

Taking Care of the Possibility of Greenwashing and Other Unacceptable Marketing Practices

Last but not least, it's critical to be mindful of the possibility of greenwashing and other unethical marketing strategies in the impact investment sector. Greenwashing is the act of claiming inaccurately or deceptively that an item or service is environmentally friendly.

To solve this problem, it's critical to extensively investigate possible investments and assess their social and environmental effects. It's also crucial to be aware of business norms and accreditations, including the Global Reporting Initiative and the UN Guidelines for Responsible Investing, which may be used to spot investments that are dedicated to social and environmental responsibility.

Aligning financial aims with social and environmental goals can be accomplished with the help of impact investment. Yet, while pursuing impact investments, investors may encounter several typical difficulties, such as juggling financial aims with social and environmental goals, resolving conflicts of values, and avoiding the possibility of greenwashing and other unethical marketing tactics. Investors may overcome these difficulties and accomplish both their financial and social objectives by approaching impact investing with a long-term view, having a defined set of principles and criteria for selecting investments, and carefully studying possible investments.

CHAPTER FIVE

Putting money toward your values in the long run

A sustainable and long-lasting future is another goal of investing in your beliefs, in addition to having an influence now. The potential advantages of long-term value-based investing are discussed in this chapter, along with tips on how to stay true to your values as you navigate the constantly shifting investment landscape. We will also look at how to develop a long-term investment strategy that is in line with your values.

Making an Investing Plan for the Long Term That Reflects Your Values

It takes careful consideration and deliberate action to develop a long-term investing plan that is consistent with your principles. It begins with figuring out how your primary principles and beliefs fit with your financial objectives.

You may start looking for assets that support your beliefs after you have a firm knowledge of them. This can entail excluding businesses that don't fit your criteria or investing in funds created with your ideals in mind.

It's crucial to keep in mind that diversity is a necessary component of long-term investment in your ideals. You may lower risk and make sure that your portfolio stays consistent with your beliefs over time by distributing your assets across a variety of industries and asset classes.

Long-Term Value-Based Investing's Possible Rewards

Long-term investment in your values might offer a variety of possible advantages. You can promote change and help build a more sustainable future by investing in businesses and funds that are dedicated to social and environmental responsibility.

Long-term value-based investing may also pay out financially. Several businesses that place a high priority on social and environmental responsibility also exhibit great long-term financial performance. You might be able to accomplish both your financial and social objectives by investing in these businesses.

Maintaining Your Values as You Navigate the Always Shifting Investing Landscape

It's crucial to adhere to your beliefs as you navigate the always-shifting financial market. This can entail frequently reviewing your portfolio to make sure it is consistent with your beliefs despite market changes.

Maintaining contact with the businesses and funds you invest in is also crucial. You can encourage good change from the inside and make sure that your investments continue to be in line with your beliefs over time by clearly defining your values and expectations.

Finally, it's crucial to understand that making a long-term investment in your beliefs is not a one-time thing. Instead, it's a continuous process that needs continual care and work. You may continue to effect change and contribute to a more sustainable future by staying true to your beliefs and keeping up with the most recent trends and advancements in the impact investing industry.

Conclusion

Long-term investment in your beliefs is a potent strategy to effect change and help build a more sustainable future. You may accomplish both your financial and social objectives by developing a long-term investing plan that is consistent with your values, diversifying your portfolio, and staying active with your assets. Long-term value investing may also provide several other advantages, such as cash gains and the satisfaction of knowing that your investments are changing the world. In the end, investing in your values over the long haul is a continuous process that calls for continuing care and work, but the benefits may be substantial and permanent.